Awaken Your Divine Wisdom

A Guided Journal Expedition to Explore Your
Universe & Decode Its Secrets

Crystal Cockerham

Title: Awaken Your Divine Wisdom: A Guided Journal Expedition To Explore Your Universe & Decode Its Secrets

Author: Crystal Cockerham

Copyright © 2020 by Crystal Cockerham

ISBN: 978-1-79489-343-6

Learn more about Crystal at www.WisdomAwakens.com

Published by: Quiet Rebel Bureau - www.QuietRebelBureau.com

Dear Wisdom Seeker,

Welcome to this guided expedition into your universe to awaken your divine wisdom.

This journal with its accompanying meditations was created to help you dance between the conscious and subconscious parts of your mind to transform those limiting beliefs into limitless ones. It is this transformative process which unlocks those pearls of wisdom that enable you to dance awake your divine wisdom and trust your personal truth.

I have designed this bundle so that you can use it again and again until you are living your life on your terms from your sovereign self free of the world's perceptions and expectations of you.

Let Your Light Shine!

Sincerely,

Crystal Cockerham

Founder, WisdomAwakens.com

Contents

7

HOW TO USE THIS JOURNAL

8

CREATING YOUR SACRED SPACE

9

SELF CARE IS KEY IN THE TRANSFORMATIONAL
PROCESS

11

THE DISCOVERY

29

THE CALLING

57

THE AWAKENING

73

SACRED CONTRACT OF SELF DEDICATION

How to use this Journal

This journal was created to aid you on your expedition of awakening your divine wisdom. I have designed it so that you begin by creating your sacred space, schedule your sacred time, do the meditation and then move to the journal.

Each section has a meditation that accompanies it. There is no harm in repeating the meditations as you need to.

I have purposely included a blank page at the end of each section for you to print off as many extras as you need. That was the most difficult part of this project, (believe it or not), not knowing how much room to leave you for your thoughts, feelings, drawings, collages & doodles, etc.

I would also suggest getting a special folder or binder to keep this in. Most of all, don't forget to add that element of fun, use colored ink, pencils, paints, etc., to make it yours!

Creating Your Sacred Space

Do you have a pre-designated sacred space?

Are you new to meditation? Before you get started, be sure that the space you intend to use is clear of clutter and is somewhere you won't be distracted by your surroundings or disturbed by others. Most often, you think of meditation and the vision of someone sitting straight up with their legs crossed in front of them comes to mind. I actually recommend for these guided meditations that you focus more on comfort. Laying down is perfectly fine. Other things to keep in mind and have on hand:

- 45-60 minutes dedicated time
- Your cell phone not in the room or set to airplane mode
- Your journal and writing utensils
- Your audio of the meditation
- Essential oils or scented candle
- Crystals or other spiritual items you are accustomed to
- Blanket for comfort
- Eye pillow should it be too bright to fully relax
- Water to stay hydrated

Self-Care is Key in the Transformational Process

Very often it goes unsaid that all types of personal or spiritual growth and transformation work is an energetic detox. I believe that if you know it in advance, it is easier to manage.

You may find that at times you have some emotional ebb & flows, spurts of energy, flux in appetite, etc.

THIS IS NORMAL.

BE GENTLE with yourself as you move through this process. I have included some tips to help you:

- Stay hydrated. Drink lots of water
- Healthy, whole-food diet
- Make sure you get ample quality sleep
- Salt baths with essential oils
- Walk/time in nature DIY/gardening/home projects (these types of projects, for me, help me to process, reflect and clear my energy.)
- Coaching/mentoring-personal guidance
- Body work
- Energy clearing

The Discovery

"The real voyage of discovery consists not in seeing new landscapes, but in having new eyes."
~ Marcel Proust

Listen to the audio track:

The Discovery

You can listen online or download the audio track from:
http://wisdomawakens.com/divine-wisdom-meditations/

The password is AwakeningWisdom

Welcome back from your inner landscape! Let us begin at the beginning, shall we?

The first you place you visited was the theater room. With as much detail as possible describe &/or sketch what you remember of this space. What did it look like? What did your seat look like? Was it cozy? What did you smell? Etc.

Describe/sketch the mossy -covered bridge. What did it feel like to step through the screen and walk on it? What noise did it make? What was the scenery like?

Once you crossed the bridge, there was a door or gate which granted you access to your inner landscape. What was it made of? What Color was it? Was there a symbol/picture/design on it? Sketch it here.

Your inner landscape resides within your subconscious mind and is created by all aspects of your being and evolves as you evolve.

As you stepped through your door or gate you found yourself on an elevated height. Describe, sketch, collage with as much detail as possible everything you remember from this viewpoint.

Were there natural, unnatural, man-made, magical or other worldly elements here?

What time of day was it? What season of the year was it?

What type of bodies of water were there? What do you smell? What kinds of beings/animals do you sense, see or hear? Are they earthly, magical &/or other-worldly?

Within this world your subconscious has created for you, you have many abilities you don't have in the earthly realm. Truly, you have any and all super & magical power you choose at your disposal. What came to mind for you here?

Which ones gave you the most delight?

Which ones, if any, gave you a bit of fright?

During this visit to your inner landscape, you were guided to take the form of a winged being. What type of winged one were you?

How does this super-power feel? And, what does the air smell like?

From this perspective, what can you see now that you didn't before? Add to your previous sketch/collage or create a new one from this viewpoint.

You entered your inner landscape to become aware of those aspects of your being that are calling you to consciously interact with them. The mist represents those aspects of you. Add to your sketch/collage now the misty areas.

As the winged one, you allowed one of these aspects of your being to draw you closer so that you could retrieve the recording of its fragmented memory. When you landed, what did you land on, a tree? a boulder? a rooftop? the ground?

Now describe the area where you landed. What did you see? What did you smell? How did you feel? Etc.

When you landed, you landed just outside the mist, when you peered into it, where in your body did you feel resistance or heaviness? Describe the physical feeling.

What feelings surfaced for you?

What sounds did you hear? Were there voices? Fragments of conversation? Music?

If you heard voices, what was being said? Try to recall and record all you can here; what happened, who said what to who about whom?

Which memory beckoned you?

What age is this aspect of your being? What was this aspect of you wearing?

How did this aspect of you feel during and after this memory?

What was going on in the background, etc?

Once you returned to the theater, you were presented with a slide show by this other aspect of your being. It showed you those moments when you have experienced the same feeling as the original fragmented and unprocessed memory you retrieved on your first journey into your inner landscape. These are the moments where you acted from the false sense of yourself rather than the truth of who you know yourself to be. You were then asked to reflect upon these moments, that feeling and the original fragmented memory you retrieved to discover the common thread. This common thread is the limiting belief that created this false sense of self. If it helps, make a list of these moments.

What is the limiting belief? Distill it down to a phrase or sentence.

You have been doing a great job! Remember to pace yourself and take care of yourself. Right now would be an excellent time to pause.

I call this reflect and process time. I am sure you need to eat or grab a cup of tea. Go about your routine and come back to this later or tomorrow.

When you return, read over what you have recorded in this sacred journal. Revisit the Guided Meditation if you feel called to do so. If you have remembered more around this memory, add it to what you have already written.

For this part of your story, this unprocessed, fragmented memory, is asking you to re-examine it, process it, re- interpret it. To rewrite it.

After you have revisited your previous entries, amend them as you need to.

Since your first journey into your inner landscape, has this false sense of self you identified been more noticeable?

Have you noticed how the limiting belief has woven itself into your everyday life? Explain.

How have you been feeling in general; sleepy, restless, emotional? Explain.

Your notes

"Nourishing yourself in a way that helps you blossom in the direction you want to go is attainable, and you are worth the effort."
~ Deborah Day

How are you doing with nurturing yourself throughout this process? Remember at the beginning I mentioned how Being GENTLE with yourself and allowing time for SELF-CARE is key in the transformational process. Each time you find yourself in a process, it is different.

One thing to keep in mind is the allowance of down time for self-care & NURTURing. You are doing some deep spiritual work and detoxing your energy. Feeding your body some healthy foods, staying well hydrated, yoga, walking, soaking in the tub, & swimming, just to name a few, are all great for helping you through this process!

Also, allowing yourself some sacred time for creative flow, whatever that is for you; drawing/painting, coloring, crafting, sewing/crocheting, cooking/baking, etc., are SOOTHing for YOUR SPIRIT and offer a space for you to have clear communication with your higher self.

And, allow yourself extra journaling time. These are your sacred pages, print off as any blank ones as you need for yourself, and when you are ready, proceed to the next meditation.

The Calling

"It is by going down into the abyss that we recover the treasures of life. Where you stumble, there lies your treasure."
~ Joseph Campbell

Listen to the audio track:

The Calling

You can listen online or download the audio track from:
http://wisdomawakens.com/divine-wisdom-meditations/

The password is AwakeningWisdom

Welcome back from your Sacred Pool. A lot went on while you were in that space and time. This next section is set up to help you recall and add to your experience.

When you are in your movie theater, you are guided through an exercise of emptying your mind. You have done this at least twice now. What have you noticed? What pops up for you on the screen? Is it the same distractions, to-do's, or thoughts each time? Take note here about this discovery so that you are aware. [It is these things that keep us from stilling our mind and also keep us in our habits and patterns, so it is good to take notice.]

*"So it is, so it will be, and it will
be so with Grace and Ease."*
~Your Higher Self

Once you emptied your mind, your inner voice asked you if you were willing to carry out this deed for both this aspect of yourself as well as your future self, and to trust that by entering this space to complete this task you were acting in your highest and greatest good and ended with the above quote. How did this sit with you? What thoughts came up in your mind around this? Did you trust in the task ahead of you despite not knowing how it was to unfold?

Upon the screen appeared the pages from your journal where you had recorded the experience of your first journey into your inner landscape. You were asked to tap into that feeling and allow it build before stepping onto the mossy- covered bridge. What was that like for you?

Once you crossed over the bridge, had the door or gate changed at all or did it remain just as you remembered?

Once you re-entered your inner landscape and remembered that you had special abilities here, had any come to mind that you wanted to 'try out'?

Did you find it easy or difficult to continue to hold that feeling?

Once you returned to your inner landscape and took flight, you were guided to take flight as a winged one through a process of release. How was that for you? Describe as much as you can here for yourself including the buildup of the emotion, the calling out, the dive, the cleansing in the water, etc.

Recall also how you felt after as you were floating atop the water. Where did you feel the new space? How was it different?

Do you feel that there may be more? (Remember, you can revisit this meditation as many times as you need to clear & release. Remember too that you have options on your secrets to self-care list that are also helpful.)

Sketch/Describe in detail your Sacred Pool of water and how it felt to be there.

After floating there a bit, and taking in the peaceful scenery, you found yourself smiling, how did that feel?

You were then guided to swim in the water for a bit, how did the water feel as you moved? How did your body feel?

Describe how the earth felt once you stood in the water.

Recall now, that moment you were standing in the water, you moved your fingertips in front of you, and you heard your Higher Self whisper: *"Look now, look to recall some of those times where you lived from that false sense of yourself as a result of this fragmented memory. Look not so that you feel poorly once more, but look so that you see the lesson, look so that you find the wisdom you need to lay down this limiting belief and false sense of self once and for all. Look too so that you receive what your past self needs to know in order to be freed from this false sense of self and make the fragmented memory whole..."* Record what you saw below.

What is the wisdom you need to lay down this limiting belief and false sense of self once and for all? What was it that your past-self needed to know in order to be freed from this false sense of self and make the fragmented memory whole?

Again, distill it down to one phrase. (Transform that limiting belief into a limitless one!) Write it here.

How did it feel to both speak those words aloud and hear those words this aspect of you has been longing to hear for so long?

"We shall not cease from exploration and the end of all our exploring will be to arrive where we started and to know the place for the first time.
~ T.S. Eliot

You have just heard your **Higher Self** tell you that now you need to deliver this message to the other aspect of your being. You go to open your eyes and before you is the reflection of that place where you retrieved the fragmented memory. You move toward it and suddenly found yourself there. **What did you make of that? What name would you give to this form of travel?**

Upon returning to this place you noticed the mist, although still there was lessened. The mist lessened because you processed the emotions of this memory. Had anything else changed since you were last here?

As you began to see the fragmented memory flicker, what came up for you? How did it feel to be able to step into the memory and deliver this message of divine wisdom she most needed to hear, feel and know in that moment?

Now, having delivered the message to your previous self, and watching her claim her power you see that the mist is cleared and how that impacted your inner landscape. How does that make you feel now and empower you moving forward with other fragmented, unprocessed memories?

Describe & Sketch this place now and include in the sketch your blossom still planted in the ground.

What type of flower was it? What color? How did it smell?

You sniff the aroma of the flower and find yourself transported back to your sacred pool and giggled with delight to find yourself standing on the shore. Is there anything you would like to reflect on or remind yourself about THIS magical means of transportation or this space?

"Go Forth Dear One, The Flame Beckons You."
~Your Higher Self

The element of fire symbolizes transformation. Every piece of the process throughout these meditations has been powerful in your transformational process. The Ethereal Fire is no exception. Sketch/describe this fire and the circle of stones.

Once you reached the fire, you saw the sacred pages of your journal and were instructed by your inner voice to burn them. As you watched them burn, what were you thinking?

What were you feeling?

The next action you were guided to take at your ethereal fire, was a process of de-chording. By pulling these chords, you are energetically banishing all the residual energy attached to that limiting belief and false sense of yourself. You were guided to view this process and these chords like a magician's scarf. How was this process for you? Try now, for yourself to describe in as much detail, every aspect of this process including where the chords were attached in your physical body, the color(s) of the scarf, how the flame reacted to them etc.

How was it for you to heal yourself in this way? Describe the difference in your physical being now from before you went through this process.

When you turned from the ethereal fire towards the shore, you felt:

Did you twirl or dance?

You then ran into and dove into the water once more. How was this for you this time?

When you emerged from the water a winged one once more, how was your flight?

"Gratitude is an antidote to negative emotions, a neutralizer of envy, hostility, worry, and irritation. It is savoring; it is not taking things for granted; it is present-oriented."
~ Sonja Lyubomirsky

Before opening the gate and stepping onto the mossy covered bridge there was a moment of gratitude. Take a moment and expand upon that by writing a 'Thank You' note to yourself here.

"Your mind knows only some things. Your inner voice, your instinct, knows everything. If you listen to what you know instinctively, it will always lead you down the right path."
~ Henry Winkler

Communicating with and trusting your inner voice is the foundation of everything in your spiritual well being. How has this communication been for you throughout this process so far? Is this new for you? Have you heard or felt this voice before? If so, did you act upon the guidance you were given?

"You have done a most excellent job today dear one. Remember, even though you have accomplished these tasks within your inner landscape, you will notice its effects in the physical world. Take great care of your physical body and look after your emotional welfare.

You have detoxed your energy centers by releasing and detoxing emotions that had been encoded in your DNA.

Take care of yourself. Sleep, hydrate, eat good healthy food and be gentle with yourself if you find that you are a little 'touchy' as these are remnants and echoes of the fragmented memory and false sense of self leaving you. You have made this memory and aspect of your being whole. Allow yourself some quiet time with her as you integrate this newfound wisdom into your being."

~ Your Higher Self

"Communing with your Higher Self and trusting your intuition is your birth right, your superpower!"
~ Crystal Cockerham

Here is your space to declare to your Higher Self your commitment to communicating with her regularly. Take this space and begin shaping what that looks like for you and begin exploring the possibilities it holds for you.

Your notes

You have been doing an incredible & courageous job! Remember self-care is key in the transformation process and critical at this particular point of the journey. Right now would be an excellent time to pause.

I call this reflect and process time. I am sure you need to eat or grab a cup of tea. You have moved a lot of energy, so now would be an excellent time to take a scented salt bath &/or spend time in nature. Then, go about your routine and come back to this later or tomorrow.

When you return, read over what you have recorded here in this sacred journal. Revisit the meditation(s) if you feel called to do so or take yourself back to the parts you need to repeat. Add any new thoughts or ah-ha's, especially if you had a dream related to this experience, to what you have already written.

After you have revisited your previous entries and amended them as you see fit, proceed to the final meditation.

The Awakening

"The journey of life is the unification of fragmentation. Fragments are units of power that are out of control. We make agreements to come and collect ourselves."
~ Caroline Myss

Listen to the audio track:

The Awakening

You can listen online or download the audio track from:
http://wisdomawakens.com/divine-wisdom-meditations/

The password is AwakeningWisdom

Welcome back from your third visit into your inner landscape. As you move through these pages you will be prompted to recall your experience just as you had before.

As you move through this final leg of the journey, keep the above quote in your mind and at the end, allow yourself to marinate on it and your experiences with this sacred journal before recording your thoughts.

Whilst in the movie theater, did you wonder why your Higher Self didn't speak to you?

As you were crossing the bridge, you were asked to pause and tune in. What sounds did you hear that you had not noticed before?

What scent(s) did you take note of?

What did you notice about your surroundings while on the bridge that you hadn't before?

Once inside the gate, you were guided to use any super power you wished to transport yourself to the shore of your sacred pool. Record that experience with as much detail as you can here.

Upon arriving at the shore of your Sacred Pool, what did your surroundings look like? Were they the same or different from when you were last there? What scents fill the air? Describe with as much detail as you can recall. Sketch if you are called to do so.

What were you wearing?

As you walked the water's edge, what did you hear? See? Smell? Feel?

"Welcome back dear one. I know you had expected
me back in the theater, and I was there with you just
as I am always with you. You are learning to trust yourself
dear, and so I needed to give you
that space to find your way here."
~ Your Higher Self

As you contemplated your newer found deep knowing and strengthening this relationship with your higher self, what do you want this relationship with your Higher Self to look like?

How can you strengthen this sacred bond that is your birthright along with gaining more trust in yourself?

How can you practice this consistently to where it becomes automatic and can be utilized as a deep source of personal power?

"Let this be the symbol of the wisdom
you have awakened for yourself."
~Your Higher Self

Describe or sketch everything you can remember about the necklace you found and its captivating beauty.

How did it feel to put the necklace on? What thoughts ran through your mind?

Your Higher Self then spoke to you about a period of integration, and advised you to come up with a mantra, a short simple phrase or sentence that sums up how you wish to BE. What is your mantra?

In the meditation, there was a bonfire area where you went to relax and contemplate the sage advice your higher self just gave you about integrating. Sketch/Describe the scene- did you have a chair? A blanket? What were the thoughts as you processed this advice?

You spoke your mantra aloud:

The flames sizzled and a projection of your future self showing you the potential power of this mantra appeared before you. What did you see? Be sure to include all you can recall including, home life, social life and professional life.

Here is your space to write a "love' letter of gratitude to yourself and every aspect of your being about this process you have taken yourself through and what you have gained from it.

By what means did you find your way back to the point of elevation just inside the gate?

Your notes

"The journey of life is the unification of fragmentation. Fragments are units of power that are out of control. We make agreements to come and collect ourselves."
~ *Caroline Myss*

Sacred Contract of Self Dedication

I, _____, vow to honor myself and my process by staying true to myself in my highest and greatest good.

I promise to repeat my mantra:

_____as needed until it becomes automatic for me to BE in this new way.

* I will make self-care a part of my regular regime.

* I will continue to nurture the sacred bond I have with my Higher Self.

* I will continue to strengthen through practice, my newly found self-trust as a source of personal power.

* I will continue to set aside sacred-self time in my sacred space to encourage continuous growth.

* I know now that this process exists and I can utilize it again and again.

* I also know that I can enter my inner landscape any time I feel called to do so.

_____

Signed and Witnessed by Me, Myself and I

Dear Wisdom Seeker,

I have included a bonus track for you to use in order to tap into the vision you have for yourself. It guides you in and calls you back with some gentle music in between for your exploration and reconnection.

Listen to the audio track:

Bonus

You can listen online or download the audio track from: http://wisdomawakens.com/divine-wisdom-meditations/

The password is AwakeningWisdom

Please don't forget to take care of yourself. Be forgiving, patient and gentle with yourself through your integration.

Remember, the allowance of down time for self care & NURTURing. You have done some deep spiritual work and are laying a new healthier foundation for yourself. Feeding your body some healthy foods, staying well hydrated, yoga, walking, soaking in the tub, & swimming, just to name a few, are all great for helping you through this process!

And don't forget to set aside some sacred time for creative flow, whatever that is for you; drawing/painting, coloring, crafting, sewing/crocheting, cooking/baking, etc., are SOOTHing for YOUR SPIRIT and offer a space for you to have clear communication with your higher self.

It has been a privilege and an honor to accompany you on your journey. If you are wanting or in need of guidance and support at any time, you are welcome to schedule an appointment by visiting: http://www.wisdomawakens.com/contact-us/

Remember,

Let Your Light Shine!

You can find and follow me follow me on social media

https://www.facebook.com/WisdomAwakens/

@WisdomAwakens

@WisdomAwakens

You can find my other writings in the following places:

My blog at: http://www.wisdomawakens.com/blog/

As a contributing author page for ASPIREMAG.net: http://www.aspiremag.net/author/crystal-cockerham/#.Wr-%20GZGaZOi4